This Book Belongs To

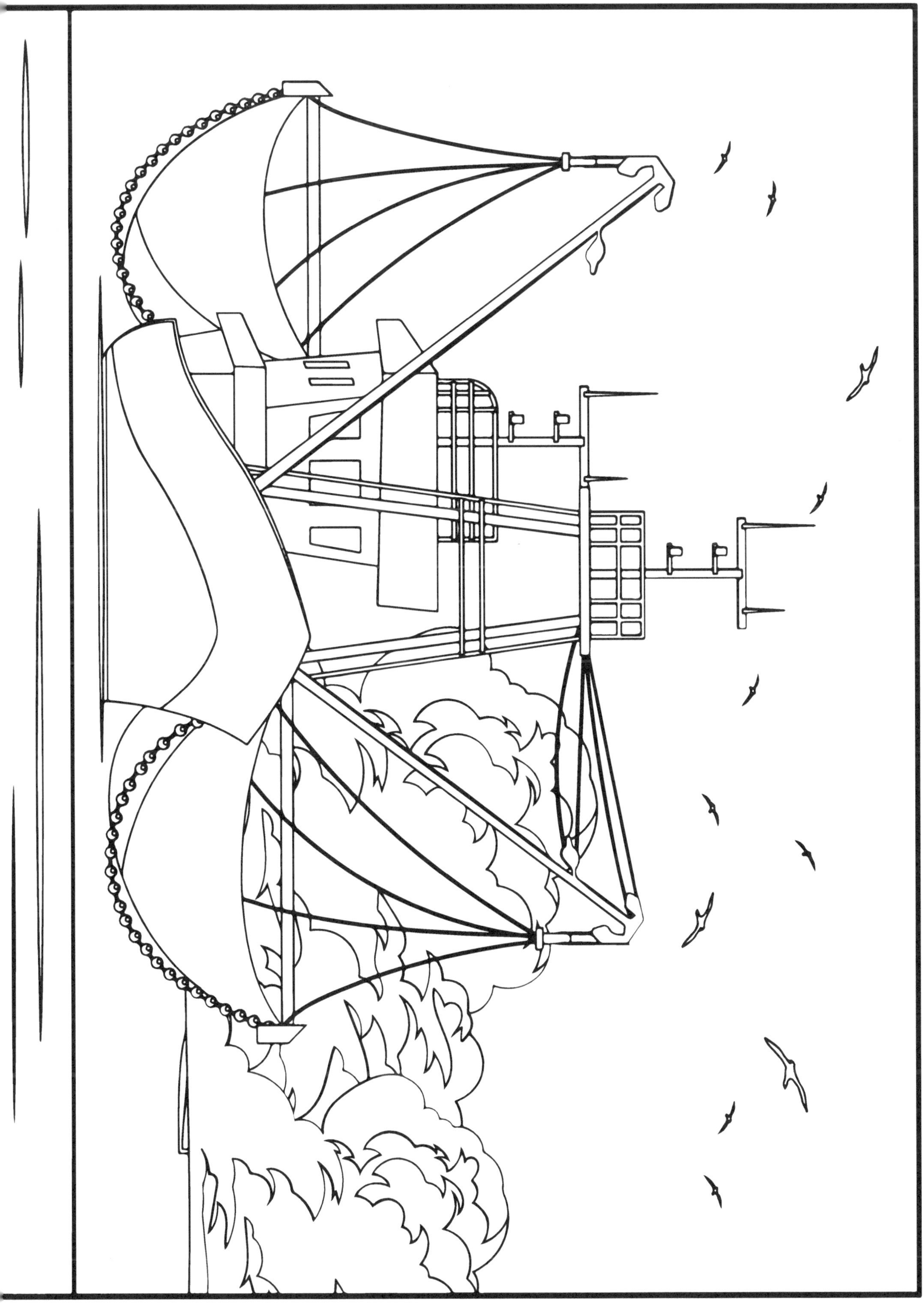

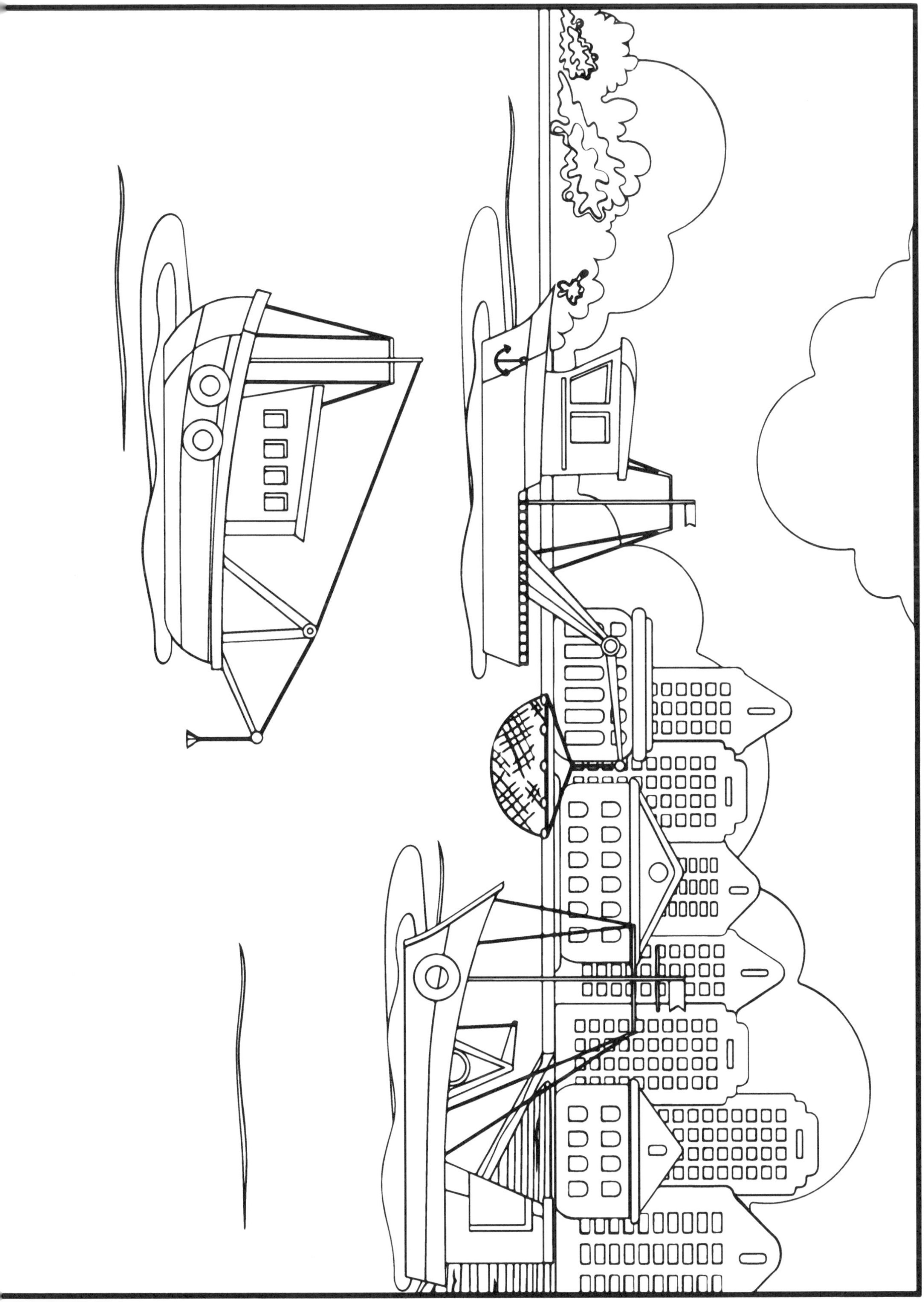

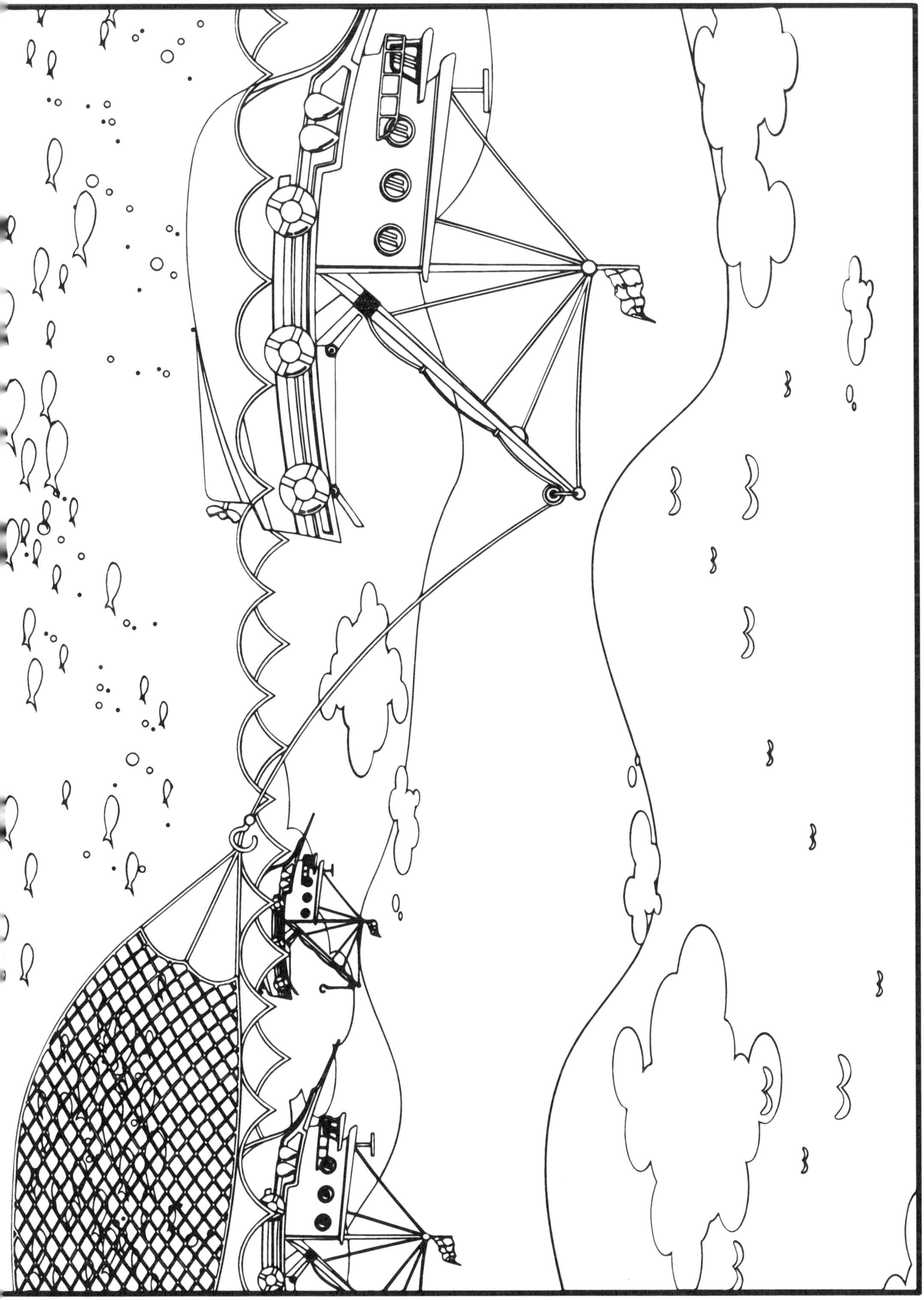

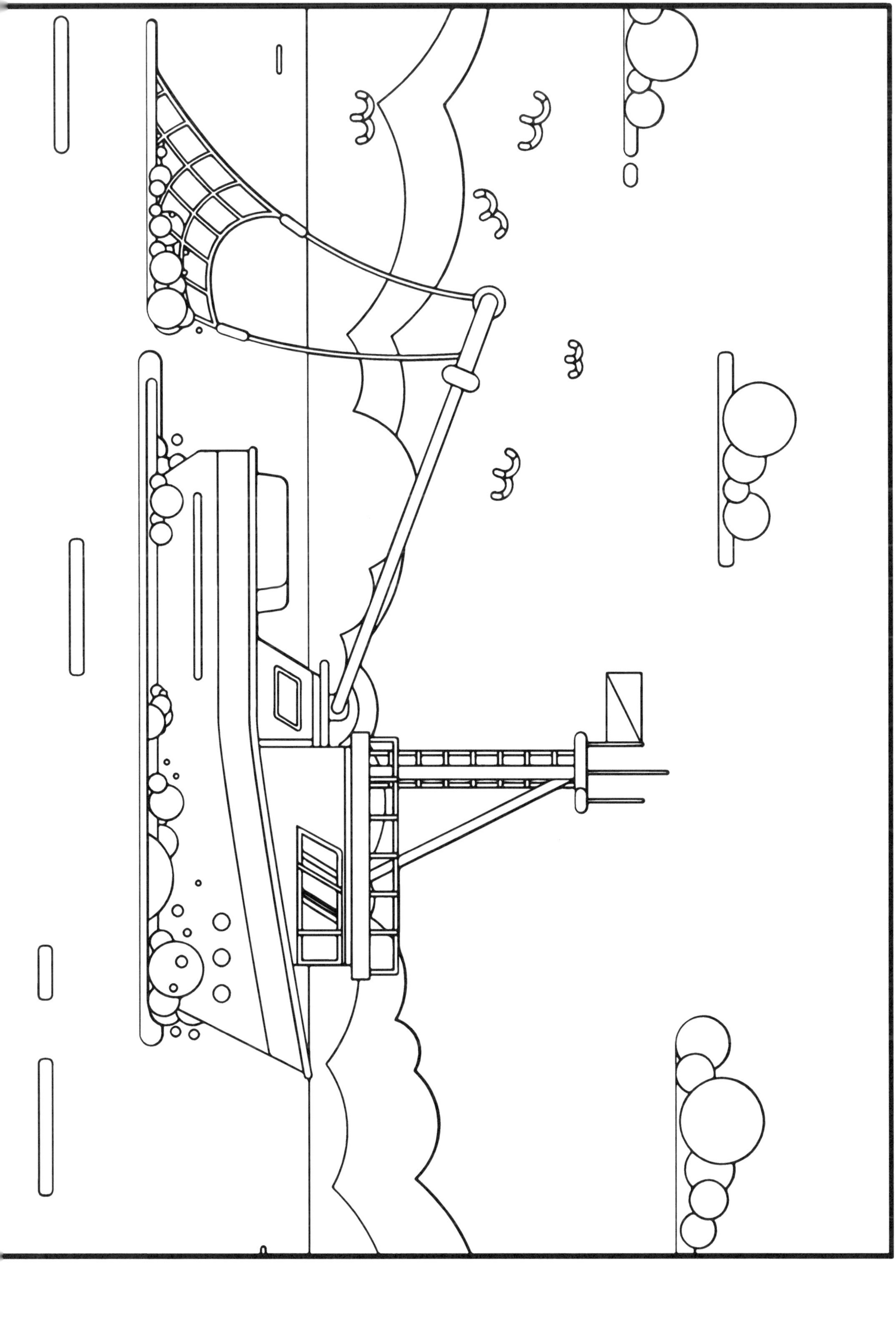

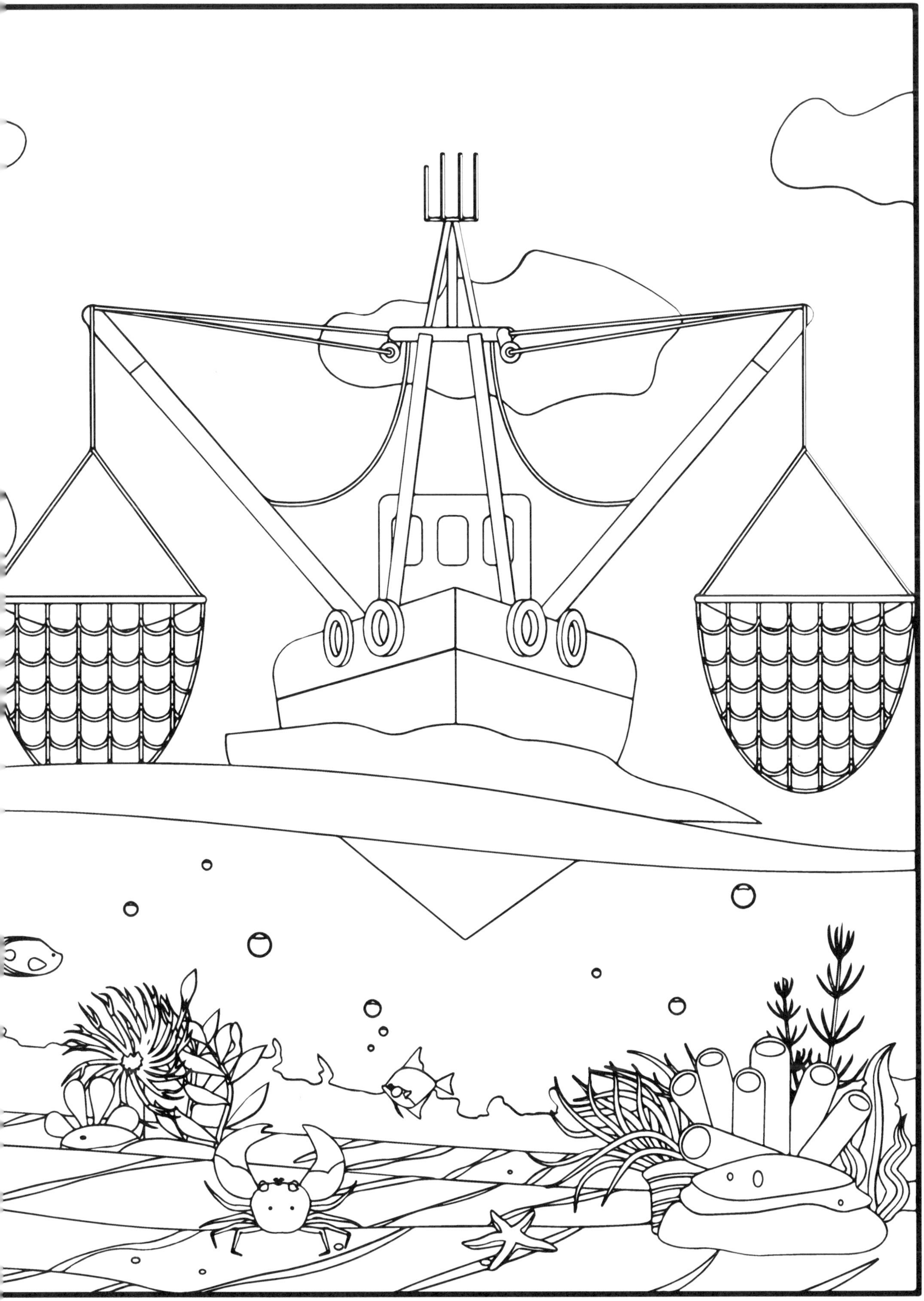

BIG
FISH

Made in United States
Troutdale, OR
07/25/2023

11543019R00038